Ágnes Lehóczky

Budapest to Babel

egg box

Budapest to Babel

First Published, 2008, by Egg Box Publishing
www.eggboxpublishing.com

Book design & artwork:
Nathan Hamilton
& Anna Mae Selby

Printed and bound by:
Biddles, Kings Lynn
www.biddles.co.uk

ISBN: 978-0-954392-06-2

egg box

BUDAPEST TO BABEL

by Ágnes Lehóczky

to Tessa Sowerby,
for her white, open house

BY THE SAME AUTHOR

ikszedik stáció (*Station X*) (Universitas, Budapest, 2000)

Medalion (*Medallion*) (Universitas, Budapest, 2002)

CONTENTS

PART 1

babel cycle

PART 2i

isn't cycle

CONTENTS

PART 2ii

Nárcisz

1

The HB pencil breaks into three pieces;
an aftermath of your disappointment...
I chose the wrong country you say,
your anger scattered around the room
like bones, dry and hollow collapses
on the carpet beside a red suitcase I found
in a fast running stream in an early spring.

babel cycle

babel 1

'confoundation'

i.

this supper's geography is malformed now look
what you sprinkled on the top avalanches to the bottom
icebergs fissured they say our foundation
breaks down to its ingredients when a plate ruptures

ii.

the drummer dropped one of his sticks twice during the performance
the others watched him pick it up from the floor waiting
an ebony double bass carried another musician on stage
on its strings a marionette to perform cacophony non stop
two saxophones inflated the lungs of the saxophonists with the kiss
of devotion at which point you and i felt the need to applaud yet our
palms could never converge could never touch, out of approval
holding on to their cocktails the audience reversed out printing
laudative silence on the rim of their glasses

iii.

the encounter with her was more than peculiar and i did not know
it was the queen they said that woke me up around four at dawn in may
i was hesitant to shroud her with a wine glass although the plan was
elaborate; the festival programme slid underneath
i suppose it was the intimacy with this agitated body yes although
i knew there was the paper to divide us

babel 2

late summer festivities; a ballad about the mason's wife

to get to the turret we climb up the spiral staircase
that echoes our disintegrating words and laughter
you drag me onto the timber boards with one hand
with the other drawing over the cadaverous skyline
the flesh-coloured tower crafted from baked bricks scaffolds

picture a tower composed of the calcium of bones
masons insisting this way it would never collapse
blending the corpse of the wife with mud-baked bricks
and look, for the seventh day they erected the bastion
– I stamp my feet to prove how safe it is

this isn't that tower, you claim, to close the subject
your embrace from behind I actually do not like
my fist in your grip pointing at the hanging gardens,
your words about our ziggurat, a bed of mortar
built and dismantled, dismantled and built overnight

babel 3

three vignettes

(caught at high tide)

no-one slept, the baby woke the house around two
his teeth must have been growing to speak one day
ears were plugged to blunt the waves of cry yet
in this vacuum no aid against the babbling of the tide

(in between wales and england swallows flash in sharp 'V')

castles and forts along the line dividing countries
on an infinite ridge we walk; and it is easier to balance
on a highway to and fro suspended in the air than on
invisible tightropes drawn between mother tongues

(as far as king's and back)

given the heavy pole it was much trickier to steer
the frail wooden vessel once let go against the gust
verbalised over and over, stupefied utterance
in vortex, meaning chafed, paddles drowned

babel 4

bbl

this moment of waking
far-off consonants
out of swooned dreams
to find fitting vowels

with language it is hard enough
but imagine the imagination
a glass of water simply
no complaints but without the glass

this is not my cat but the landlady's
a bean on a canvas just perfect
curled up like a cat
on my duvet to confound

have a bath without the tub
and landladies' language drowns
the carpet that saturates
I dry up with a vowel

babel 5

balal's journey to and fro

the movement was elementary and routine with which balal took the pair of socks out of the drawer rolled up like slugs entangled in love on a monday morning as it was chilly outside despite it being summer in england in june yes the movement was ordinary however balal drifted into meditation about the bamboozling phenomenon of unrolled material spraying sand out like lost syllables or like magma hardly audible sprinkling on the palms and the veins engraved in the palms then finally on the rug in fact the reception was slower than the motion of the grains of sand parachuting out of the socks onto the timber floor of balal's room to locate the source of the occurrence the answer gradually tiptoed in rumouring the obvious that it travelled from the mirage of the floating shoreline balal might have visited at the weekend but to carry all these fractions of sandbanks three hundred miles across the border all over to wales after surviving being spun and tumbled with ionic surfactants as far as the chains of the brecon beacons was somewhat perplexing and indeed there was a notion of the nonsense and the inexplicable in the subject matter when balal pulled the socks back on with the million crumbs like rambunctious morphemes in the warm vacuum of the mouth and climbed welsh mountains where the soil was red inevitably blending some of the spongy granules with chewy clayed particles of the native earth at which point balal might have wanted to ask *so what?* nothing! and yet spectacular and extraordinary that these grains could be carried unconsciously on the top of *pen y fan* left there abandoned for ever but does anyone know whether they would conform to the red soil that was full of iron protective military terrain while these sand grains were awash with sand and air and minerals and other crystals yet they were only flesh-coloured morsels futile like full stops in an infinite sentence or if they would yearn for gulf currents to breathe them back to the north sea… increasing perplexity balal needed to contemplate vice versa finding welsh heather in the shoes picked up on sugar loaf transporting it all along to the east coast dropped among the coarse grass of the dunes three hundred miles away from a land that was six hundred meters above the sea suspended six hundred meter vertical difference in the density of oxygen and temperament which made balal wonder how the plant would root down in the slippery particles of the dunes and who would burn it down when the season came to strengthen its stem… this cargo of geography in socks and shoes would prolong the enigma of the incident raising inarticulate questions while picking out bits of heather from the fissures of the sole shaking sand dunes out of socks until the last gram the last iota retired in a crack of the timber floorboards

babel 6

garden dialogues

we don't know the name of the plant
we want to know the name of the plant
carroty liquid streams out when we break
the stem; strange substance of meaning
I would dip my finger into
to draw my hieroglyphs on your forehead

but there is no credit in the phonemes that pour out of my mouth
shrivelled cherries half rotten papayas not worth purchasing
ok I find diphthongs embarrassing to say the way you do
lips need to be elastic slugs in the act of androgynous love
but look at these unusually shaped fruits I dare you to eat them
roll them in your sinuses and spit the pips drawing accents
on a vowel bearing *öszibarack* or *málna*; say it little by little

say it and then take a look at the tiny boy
who sits in silence on the stone floor
in the garden near a pot of flowers
reaches out for a handful of soil from time to time
to chew and then to swallow smiling with black teeth

babel 7

mother's bon voyage to an island

in mirrored exchanges of epigrammatic eyeing
I would sit between her and a torso aged her age
adamant rammed in her throat her fists secreted
in mine from 'keen spectators of an anguished life'

yet if it was that sublime syntax she would airily
pronounce 'a slice of soft ricotta with fresh white
bread', ardent to sketch her way to a byzantine dome
in her supreme stilettos pattering in a cobbled cul-de-sac

here the afternoon, overcast, would mutely fade away
with tongue-tied *tête-à-têtes*, civilities of numb coughs
while I'd translate the silence of the crisp room for
her to stir gently into a whirlpool of milky tea

babel 8

la bibliotheca total

the note lying on the kitchen table was hardly audible almost a blank page saying *please get sheets in when dry thanks* so balal glanced at the garden through the window reflecting a face almost as vacant but somewhat inquiring and panned over the eucalyptus that grew sickle-shaped leaves over the orange blossom pronouncing white petals over the tibetan prayer flags fanning mystic messages beginning with the primal sound they say decoded by the wind with faded colours drifted into the shades of summer hieroglyphs painted on the homespun fabric over the oval pond an elliptical vowel fluidly uttered a bubble blown by the atmosphere in which balal knew fidgety tadpoles crisscrossed nervously still with a tail but soon without one that made as much difference as accents on an unknown alphabet at which point balal felt the urge to investigate finding a lump of mince in the bottle green water encircled with hundreds of miniature sharks writhing and twitching hooked on their own idea of survival as if the only meaning had been accomplished… and balal wandered into the profundity of it diving into the aquatic realm of fringed yellow and green water lilies red and white water buttercups pond parsnips and ferns broad-leaved and hair-like weeds and ivy combing through the overgrown glance balal took at the willow moss anchored to stones and pebbles in the bottom of the sense of it all trying to swallow a fan-leafed crow foot or a marsh marigold waving at the nostrils gripped with a thumb and a finger lips compressed sinuses ballooned to sustain oxygen down there for a few more seconds so that balal could have a final blink at the roots of the pink speedwell said not to be a good survivor… snorting and spluttering balal's face surfaced taking a breath long awaited seeking the blue sky camouflaged as a square shaped dry blank page

babel 9

hieronymus bosch's pessimism
(from the central panel to the right wing)

and the car loaded with luggage overturned
landing into a dark ditch of thought by a single
carriageway cradled in coarse grass and hay
scarring messages on my face and on yours resting
beside mine pupils wide open dark green iris reflecting a shape

of a building blurred an optical figment of the membrane
circular like mistakes we made again and again
with a long-tailed beast climbing a swaying ladder
against a red bricked wall carrying an oval tray
of freshly mixed cement and mortar for dark skinned
workmen raising heavy floor beams with the aid of a hoist
instructed by a human sized maggot from the ground
littered with clumps of hay and twisted human limbs gnawed
genitals of cadavers female torso stripped stabbed
a hunter with a long beak searching for the dead
hounds hem in… sniffing the straw piercing the fibre
of our clothes as the rope rotating on the crane stretches…

and I freed my hand entwined in yours and pressed my palm
on your forehead slowly drawing downwards

babel 10

brueghel's optimism
(actual size detail)

if you wonder whether there is anything positive in all this

observe these microscopic details atomic fine points

sharp angled shapes of life-sized blocks of marble

wrapped in a delicate range of cream tones laterally laid

brush marks become palpable in the eclipsed areas

these rounded chubby figures, look, definitely smiling

(at this moment in time and place from where we stare)

clad in contrasting grey-green hues picking up the colours

of the ground while tiny white highlights craft the tops

of pointed punches and mallets to cut the butter soft stone

the oily yellow fibre of a garment and a bottle green hat

the woven basket in the foreground enfolding a fresh loaf or

those blood orange leather boots in perfect profile, empty portents

babel 11

adieu to m.

you ask if your hair is long enough
to drain into fine canals meandering
between sepia pebbles sunk in sand

your fluid narcissism suits you
and I wonder how long I could
hold my breath to flood the smooth

labyrinths of your ears with an
infinite sentence to hold you back...
oh give me that bottle green

t-shirt we wore stretching the feather-
stitch work of our hullabaloo
nature in the gravity of crystal

lakes your enamel face afloat
paralleling mine – spoken
in the liquefaction of air

babel 12

mother monologue

you suppose you have got nothing to say
dazed with numb pupils into the raucous
screen and I wonder what happened

to your sentences the ones you would have
silently syllable-d… the ones you were ready to
let go unborn yet curled up in the dried out

abyss of your mouth shrivelled rudiments
aborted self-definitions oh mother…
you say *nothing* shaking your beautiful head

given up reading the simple lyrics of the programme
while I search on for your mislaid words
in the house in the car in father's factory

and spot them among metallic shavings
un-welded utterances of waste… muted…
under turning lathes he left behind to oxidize

babel 13

that translucent green

that translucent green
beetle in the white bath
does not make sense
not in this language

shampooed self-forgettings
better to drain
watching the long thin legs
clinging to a globular

meaning of the metal ring
for long minutes until
the next morning glued
to the plastered ceiling

bigger and stronger
no surprise when it takes off
a shadow of a helicopter
in the enamel sky

babel 14

notes between Budapest and Babel

Kelenföld: a word with a marginal etymology, a land to cross? perhaps, each meter or inch we make, a conquest of a land to construct barriers of a language, but let's call it that for the security born from naming… in a suburban train station of the eleventh district in a loose embrace of tower blocks at the final sigh of tram 49 after the last semicircular bend, a stuttering manifesto of once elegant utterances regurgitates to a rectangular square with tiny shops like sheds, pig sties, wooden or plastic boxes that function as beer bars, fruit or food stalls selling frankfurter sausages and other specialities I cannot define in this language, at a cheap spirit bar a dog tied to a lamp post waiting for the intoxicated owner while staring each other out both wishing to swap to be… near the ticket office a peeling yellow building decorated with pigeon lofts all around, still grey atlases scaffolding a weak structure like solitary subjects in elliptical sentences such as: *WC a Posta mögött* – the sign says on cardboard and I find the toilet behind the post office, wondering if it is really there or if the construction is self-made, scratched with graffiti perhaps by the cat in the foreground munching cold meat from a bowl while two men inside are counting coins nodding at me that I may go in accepting the 50 forint coin, no paper but I wasn't expecting any

the concrete is red like the soil on the border dividing Wales and England thrown away beer cans between the rails cigarette packets and plastic bottles corroded, narow streams meandering in between footsteps on the floor and I wonder if it is urine, if we are in Ghana and start counting the endless number of cargo wagons painted rusty red too narrowing down into a dot, into the possibility of a full stop at the end of the infinite, empty, carrying nothing, yet they seem to be very heavy

I answer a misdialled call and a female voice sends me back to my mother's cunt, I put the phone down blushing and ashamed looking around to see if anyone could hear it and wait for the train… that journeys through a 100 km short distance for nearly 3 hours in the peak of the ignited summer with a few carriages packed with dogs, teenagers, old people and I wonder how many breaths can be taken sentences uttered within 180 minutes times the number of passengers on the train and remember my friends' reminder that I will smell of train after the journey and indeed train smell does exist: the amalgam of body smell and breath smell and dog smell and cigarette smell and the smell of rust and iron that creeps on the tongue and up in the palate, yes, iron, the most dominant of all turning into an acidic smell of sentences and magnetic conversations of anger and passion… I want to smell like that too

last night I saw her after ten years, where exactly was the last time I saw you? perhaps in the metro for a few seconds but we only waved then from separate carriages, blurred reflections mirages of our selves… now we talk of politics and she wants to sit right next to me in the bar not opposite and feels proud that we were both born in '76, special babies, special generation, fragile but gifted if only someone realised, ready to burst into tears both at weddings and funerals, I know, I knew

and she laughs hysterically and I notice she stutters and cannot express herself and I remember the book that warned me long ago that we do not own our mother tongue… and I start stuttering too and laughing neurotically myself and our stammering turns into a bitter whimper around midnight at the last table of the last bar with the last drink… and we skip the children's church group again and sink into underground labyrinths of the '80s, we are in Banana Republic, do you know what it means? to sell your life for a plate of lentils? we say and I wonder why that woman cursed at me on the phone when she made the mistake perhaps that is the reason, when I see you again, bring poems and we will read them out loud, you ask when the taxi stops at 2 am and I go to bed straight away, into the one where father thought of death the day before he died

the train that inaudibly rolls into the copper-coloured station, not only perfectly quiet but brand new… and I start mourning for the lost romanticism of poverty I wanted to indulge in, to surrender to the smell of rust, to these metallic syllables of despair and venom and instead this train is newly refurbished and two well-dressed elderly ladies talk quietly without any intense gestures

at least your mother showed some passion last night in her night gown before we dived into the gaudy night-life on the crumbling art nouveau Pest side… we should feel lucky she says that we had parents like her as our words are strongly built towers and we mean what we say and I notice she stutters too and weeps when she remembers the church where we used to assist the priest giggling under an overhanging gown of an angelic hangman during the offertory and so we leave your mother in eternal euphoria and sadness… do not worry you say her wrinkles smooth out when uncle Gyuri visits her twice a month for a few hours each time

… and I watch the oxidized station go by slowly dozing to the sound of the fine talk in a cradle of soft sentences… through the window I spot two storks over the lake, two forgotten orthographic signs I could no longer read written in the reeds wings open… and I notice another one and two or three more; the entire country covered with copper-beaked white storks

2

Notice that the being verb isn't is a tease, a conundrum in English and simply does not make sense? In the other tongue we have two separate words – *van, nincs* – two unattached bodies while isn't amalgamates a beast that either exists or does not or, simultaneously, both. No, certainly isn't isn't a word.

isn't cycle

i

isn't

Cargo

(for Agnes Nemes Nagy)

To encircle the mind of the metropolis you must hop from roof to roof you must arch the distance between tiled roofs to flat roofs with a seven league motion bonding the paper with the hand and measure the hiatus between each cargo wagon with the breath you take after each word running along a rail line that passes by negligible stations between open ends of an odyssey, unrestricted, that wanders along patches of orange anoraks smeared on your glass in sudden sequences like an old filmstrip stationary in motion along another journey of another fugitive sentence

to understand you must be on either side whether inside or outside the premises of the worksite humped with building rubble and heaps of scrap iron you must recycle their debris left behind for you to craft to speculate between bright yellow railway wagons freshly painted overnight a nocturnal occupation you long for colouring inestimable bodies decolouring the night posing in neon-lit depots by draughty train cars with doors left open you must indeed stand in the inner or outer draught of abandoned compartments to understand what has just escaped

and it continues until the cranes, the city's lighthouses, signal how far you have travelled to, sweeping the horizon, spotlighting their own prolonged shadows; you must home in on the cranes stuck in the core of the city encompassing the geography of the capital arcading its cryptogrammic meaning long told and left at platforms in haste and when you craft you'll craft orange anoraks zig-zagging carefully around their outlines and fulfil your days climbing up ladders leaning against lampposts repairing colouring fixing streaking revamping or kneeling on rail sleepers bending between the rails every time an inch closer to your final destination you absent-mindedly travel by after painting mending revamping in depots and factory yards following the turns of cranes the drills of dredgers passing by fields of black tyres piled on each other along the embankment padding its sloping sides along metallic fields of cans coke cans and beer-cans when you recycle it all you'll craft plastic black crows flickering on random trees then the industrial fields of yellow rubber pipes cylinders generators containers Calor gas bottles and finally the overcrowded fields of tins of paint of blue red and yellow, you must believe you are not on your own that you too will be passed by several other coloured journeys

and when almost there… an empty playground goes by your afternoon unaccustomed to children, unaware of colours, why is there, you ask, a grey coated man walking his basset hound across the park always round the hour when you pass by, as if he was erasing colours pointing at each of them one by one with his walking stick? overtaking it you must find out who designs the patterns on train cars and cargo wagons or on green tractors with yellow inner tyres of those extravagant iron yards with heaps of wreckages who shapes the waves of corrugated iron fences and directs scenes of corroding properties unveiling rusty Volvos once crisp white? your train, you'll see, always stops a hundred yards before it terminates

take a step a station closer! a thought closer towards the core of the foreign city you were seeking under here you must stay in approximations stamp with your feet on this square meter empty of bulldozers or cranes and draw a hundred and eighty degree turn in the sand towards the geometry of the hills and meadows and head backwards? homewards? outwards? towards two tractors ploughing your view in the cloud of white gulls who flew inland picking their luck under the arc of crop sprayers chained like a circular sentence slowly rolling round and round the diameter of the earth

Summer dialogues in Budapest

Monday morning trooped in with demonic thunder leaving us entrapped. I wondered how you would get to the car, while you examined the tarred sky through white net curtains and shrugged your shoulders.

*

In the heart of the 8th district you asked me how and made notes as I answered. Take the shape of a medieval maze and occasionally go backwards, don't question. Fighting with minotaurs you would get to the origo. Our pact was: we will bury each other as the signpost of friendship. Who goes first is unimportant.

*

At another table we challenged each other to define unrequited loves. We described them each as different trees: our last ones could have been a forty meter *pinus sylvestris*, a Scotch pine, a coniferous fir that reaches to the ninth sky and is the tree of the winter solstice. The trunk is resinous and easily flammable and yet among the evergreens it is the most common. So we both barked up the wrong tree.

*

In the cleft palate of the elongated street, there it stood, the cultural centre agape: Bluebeard's castle emanating unpleasant breath windows smashed, firewalls scraped with mysterious hieroglyphs, demonic graffiti claws addressing future generations with bruises; tacky tattoos on an old body. We panicked. Stupefied adults, we ran.

*

I disguised my surprise when you admitted that at your work you often improvise movie translations. Last time you had no choice; you guessed from context.

*

My grandfather eventually told me. They had been sewing their entire life; they used to watch till the red plate of the sun inflamed the horizon. The Singer rattled, the heavy flatiron steamed on the crease. Then they tape-measured my waist and established that since September nineteen ninety-nine it got wider.

Cupla focal

(At the mouth of the River Liffey)

she stops abruptly to tap the skull of Erskine Childers' death-mask;
in a dusked side-chapel of the cathedral to the right of the apsis
look at his face, it's her as a baby, her parents used to say
jolting on top of yellow double-deckers on the way to town
and I too notice the resemblance in those sternly stiff lips
when she spits slanders and curses like pips of bitter winter lemons
or when she forbids me to enthuse about this country and its jewel
she knows so little of that I have to break into manuscripts eagled glazed
and find my own way among cobbled patterns and bespectacled writers
cast in bronze in every corner leaning reflectively on walking sticks

(In Galway-bay)

you swear you'll never come back here for good dragging your old skin
through paths and alleyways gradually moulting your nationality;
you do not talk like they do as you brushed the Gaeltacht off
your tongue leaning in the mirror for long years searching for a
hygienic landscape

Nora Barnacle's jewellery was soldered and amalgamated with her
index-finger but look, your Claddagh tarnished your luck by the end
of rootless tours looped on your left hand loosely facing outward
towards the ocean

(On Inishmurray Island)

it started raining; cats scribbling about the roof for hours, persistent
like you listening to her breathing with wide open eyes but she only
listens inwards to those thirty-odd year-old pines swaying inside the
room humming of monks that left the cells; bees that abandoned
their beehives, behind the dunes only arctic terns and storm petrels
perch in sand

if we dive down to the sea-bed in the Atlantic we'll meet all
thirteen-hundred sailors; the sinuses of puffed-up faces
overflowed with green waterweeds bubbling fish

Wrought iron girder railway bridge

say Blackfriars today surfaced as some bridge crossing the Danube its light electric trains were obsolete yellow tram-cars arbitrarily shrieking improvised from the depot from downtown on rails melting into a metropolis anonymous for the fare we stick to a hundred forint coin engraved in the centre of your warm palm circular spinning geography rotating topographic wits velocity of thoughts random *tête-à-têtes* on St Paul's Walk opposite an iron bridge a wrought ornament of imagination yet exchanging rivers may not craft a home from the vagabond's global tune in the high street compressing and expanding the bellows up and down time and again

the sound of the voyage is reassuring to you although you mistake it for the winding resonance of sentences throbbing on the thick glass you press your face against, but this train, like a ghost train, is silent; we must get off here and confide in a bridge that rises in absence alongside, relics of eight cylindrical piers in progress of disintegrating; in completion of falling apart it is a bridge we must walk across we must walk across in an engineering haste re-erecting it from four sets of quadruple-clustered abutments crumbling away in the fast running river expecting the tram to arrive on time

look a wrought iron girder railway bridge is so near so close to us that the autumnal shafts refracted in the window are quasi concrete, from un-demolished platforms passengers push on and off throwing oblique shadows on the cars' ephemeral design swaying in vertigo in neon illusion; we are not on a misguided journey, waves on both river banks are suspended high in the air the carriage parades on in parallel applause; it has always been happening this tram has always been arriving, has already arrived

we have always and already known this sitting still sometimes long hours indulgently waiting for the apparition by the Thames on the Danube's bank blanking the view of a pregnant woman woken from her peripatetic slumbers Soho's ghost returning to direct us out of dark alleyways away from the fabricated routes of rail-lines; how many worlds have we exchanged? wait… we can't have missed it, we have recognised the insignia on the front we have found the tracks for the original alignment

it isn't (i)

and indeed it isn't but this fog that chokes these objects, lucid carriages drawing over the semi-circle of the bridge and I remember… a tram's everyday journey, an unmistakable particle of hydrodynamics trapped above the river – coloured nought… it made me forget about that imaginary hillside I crawled up among imagined pines sketching the conduit of your acidic breath to the peak for a washed-out need to make sense of these irregular attachments and detachments after trudging on so many season-less paths… look how these contradictory climates drain all complexion of coats and expectations for a hued horizon of vacant faces who breathe on fluid windows of trams lost in sightless vista simply white

it isn't (ii)

the escape to the allotment was swift on bikes on a winter Sunday afternoon after your eternal weekend visit to the home the clouds hung low and inky and the sketched pear tree paralysed on your return we talked of losses and what it means to come from the so far-off past that death could become a drowsy sigh of a wish and worms erupt out of the soil as forks dig in for untamed plants… the pig you used to take for a walk left you and the white-washed sty agape with the weight of nostalgia on your chest for a journey shepherding scraping it with a twig and letting it plunge into random piles of acorns and chestnuts; strutting back on the path to the old house we find she too has fled after somersaulting down a final hill sliding nonchalantly into a lake tinted white

it isn't (iii)

today is irreversibly cold and the windscreen floods
with sheep after an unexpected bend you need to slow
down for a sudden wave of white that tides our bonnet
offsetting the car from its axis all the way through
trusting that what is beyond the glass is beyond our
reach of any menacing turns or traps and I can vaguely
register your muffled thrill about your patients mostly
about the boy who does not respond to his name and I
too can see as much correlation between these woollen
clouds and the ones in the rear-view marching gradually
into a dot or what is between my finger and the print it
leaves on glass (look for years I thought you owed me
happiness but the thought tips all at once like the content
of a bin between a Monday and the wall and I beg to
return that strangely colossal key to an imagined shed I
used to carry in my right pocket to and fro on lunatic days)

Further contemplations on 'is'

This fabula is about the Chameleon who was incredibly versatile.
She could become who ever she wanted
depending on who wanted what.
On Monday she was an ancient weary branch
of a baobab tree and let all the wasps and wild bees
make nests in her arm pits.
Other days she appeared to be the clay-coloured soil
breeding a fertile environment for the dung beetle
who got accustomed to rolling its dodgy content over her body.
She felt so empathetic with the humming bird's sorrows
that she was convinced getting drunk with him from the juicy nectar
would be a good point in their friendship.
And she carried on like this day by day in the hope of becoming.

Ecology of the lichen

We paddle head over ears in a field of yellow flowers,
with only heads surfaced in an unplanned discourse,
attuned, swimming in meadow, meandering among
old crypts and tombs. I mistrust their shapes, their
sepulchral postures made of bath stone, chalked

extravaganza. You can tell, I haven't yet wrapped bodies
in linen, you smile. It gives a shape *like that*, and facing
me you cut a sarcophagus out of the moist air crafting
a swift choreography of a corpse, outlining my outline.
These lime stones are hollow, look. We stare through

their tunnels, sliding our hands in their craters for names
and dates, for one or two initials; but none. Have you,
have you done it before? In the bare space only a slice
of a face, fraction of a glare, mouth half open, your voice
slips through. You laugh. Who do you think prepares them?

You dip your finger into a soft headstone coated with deep
pigments of lichen, orange, red and brown. Like a catacomb's
network, complicated under the microscope's lens. They live
with their photosynthetic partner – you say brushing yellow
pollen off my skin – who produces food for them from sunlight.

Map of dislocations

the journey is long and smooth the vista
swift and yellow there is a dead woman on
the train but no-one notices her open
foggy eyes wandering on the ceiling or her
thin lips crumpled like those chains of
mountains you saw from the plane – your
first flight; for some reason you all think
she is reading the paper with her glasses on

I plunge in details: the intolerable ones
from time to time, in the image of a nun
tiptoeing in a pair of red patent leather
shoes on her way to mass on a warm spring
Sunday morning treading in a puddle of
blood while she forces my eyes upwards
with endless interrogation

I say farewell at night from the top of a hot
concrete block near the airport running
down the stairway I stumble on a white
haired man lying on the landing you stand
up there inaudibly outside your door waiting
for me to notice him; your whisper trickles
down the stairs: *leave him, he sleeps there every*
night, just go…

you don't notice that the glass you drink
from is a magic one: always full, after the
fifth one you threaten me that I'll never find
another one and I too feel obliged to accept
a drink from the old Serbian émigré who
knows the *w* is impalpable in *Norwich* and

says *we* when he talks of Manchester United… so I too decide to knock back this crystal poison made of pure pears with no added sugar

near the Mediterranean your yells rhythmically wave in the phone *get out of the water, there's a massive shark coming* or *out of the sea, it's April, your eardrum will explode on the plane back* simultaneously training your third child in you *look, we are meant to be born where we are* you mechanically add

did you not hear that five thousand rabbits got released on the M1 in your country as a truck tipped yesterday? you ask straight away on my return, like a wounded beast it fell you think out loud while I replace the keys to that old apartment with the one to a street-less house, detached, shove my passport and the season ticket for the metro into the drawer

Zero milestone; St Paul's

you all know here, you consent, what poetry is up to all three of you around this table know when it strikes just as the skins of the garlic a crushed nestling's feathers blow up when you breathe out a smile too sudden and say here is the metaphor easy… look… white

two… five… nine… shuffling steps up circular height an elderly couple whisper curly *I love you*-s into the wall precisely thirty-two steps from each other smiling and waving… oh dome-shaped love how easy, if only you were here to test if it works – that there were a dome in our forehead too that could make this secular spiral worship grow simply by distance

you cut a slice of bread on the hardened wooden board and burn the toast then you retry; you singe the slice again incising the loaf carefully waiting for it to brown then burn – this is how it all starts, the story of perpetual slicing and burning bread until it becomes charcoal you can write with, now, easy, just so remarkably so

the choice, squeezed between the pinnacle and the crypt, to enjoy a coffee with the dead is neither comfortable nor cosy yet I'd spend the rest of my life in the warm nooks of the apses or wandering round the cupola my profile in sunlit exchange of semi-circled whispers where it is ok to overhear to eavesdrop in the gallery of affections for all visitors and I too may randomly experiment with the echoing acoustics of misanthropic love is it geometry that scaffolds this city's make-up and posture? iron bars and solitary cranes heavy headedly nodding at midnight swinging signalling the route back home to the round table of light metaphors no sweat… in a city that starts when height is built sky-scrapers of internationality upright it starts from where an addict chewing dodgy plants on a tube to the suburbs becomes composition

November meals on wheels

An atypical ringtone. Your falling cadences. The family is well;
quiet but not surprised. She was found in the kitchen two days
after your last visit, lying on the floor in her patterned gown,
her dinner can hanging on the door since Monday, unattended.

You are there; I am here, and this here and there is so well-defined
that no metaphysics can fuse them into one world yet you want
identical autumn, identical time zone, identical region of the earth;
that hour matters. It is everything. All our belongings are in that hour
dissected in three-thousand and six hundred seconds.

That hour is in-between. There's no overlap but in the solar time
in that interval between two successive returns of the sun.
I too have been preparing for a cycle ride for years. Planning a route
back to the meridian, round an imaginary circle. Watching the satellite
for snow. Muffling all footpaths. Snowing up windscreens of maps.

I am sorry to hear your grandmother's dead. Have you thought
of those happenings in-between? She may have tripped. Hit her head.
Have you thought of that suspicious distance? That arc faded between
the upright and the floor tiles. Two days' secret of her life. Let it be.
No, there is no sign of intrusion, nothing's been taken;
the flat stands the same.

En route

Have you, right the way through, stood in this garden? In
the very inside of mid spring. At the junction of hectic air-

routes of assiduous bugs. A few thoughts after an abrupt
shower. After you buried certain attachments – that wearing

yet necessary open-air occupation. All this time? Fixed in
the hold of neighboured houses, tiled triangular roofs, walls

crafted from ivy and birds' ad hoc nests, impromptu imaginings.
Semi-sensing the draught roused by the scream of a single

gull quasi smoothing your hair for only a moment, introvert,
like a soul of some body with a dislodged self-direction.

Is this unquestionably the place you have been up till now?
In the autonomy of the square. Inside the garden; outside.

Photographs, undeveloped

Somewhere a tourist book was warning the reader that this capital was grey. I depicted it. I saw a grey childhood. Swinging the Soviet Horizont in one hand wandering amongst art nouveau houses shooting around down town. Under arches of courtyards black and white: those films I have never developed. What I mean is I have never taken them to the shop. I did not need to. What I mean is I did not need to see them at all.

My mother in that other era used to sit on the roof drawing the passing sky on her own. Her hair was thin, uncut, colourless. She needed to climb up the ladder to get up there to the loft and from there to the top onto the tiles. Later she used colours. But in that era those colours became neutral on the paper; I don't mean decolorized. That era was neither toneless nor grey. It was a thick white glass. Through that glass was my mother observing those clouds, I think.

Much later, in another millennium, I saw those galleries on a poster. The grey capital's apartments on sale. But it was in a different country. What I mean is that it happened in another century. What happened in another century in another country? I think it is 'it' I talk of that occurred then between the black and the white. If anything this capital is in-between. It is painted naught, or it was. Light yellow, in January, when you look out of the train pulled by the rails, no, not too fast.

Why were we both disloyal? What I mean is why do we not live in the place, no matter where, that we actually live in? We meet here three times a year waiting for each other behind bins lining the dark at night. It is cold. A January. A January just before Christmas is what I mean. It is such a Christmas is what I mean. Those bins happen at each corner. One after another you hide from me and ask me to do the same for you. There is no plan in the future and so you leave the country on Christmas day.

Take the train to the border. What I mean is that border drawn between two pine-trees. They are pines of the same woods, of the same pine. In-between; take a walk in *tomb-land* where veterans of the Alps, of the same land of the same woods, still assemble from time to time. The bones used to be scattered. Sporadically. I see. Now… martially renovated stones… I fit my soles in your traces on a path of our sledge you used to pull in the snow. Forgive me if I don't spend any more time with you here. What I mean is don't I spend more time with you spending time with ghosts?

Don't blame the signs of the galleries in St Paul's. What I mean is there are no circular walls that could bring those voices back. We left them there in that discoloured era. Or is it that they only whisper in that white coloured glass? Leave the domes' troubles to the domes. And the trams' to bridges that can hold them no longer. I think domes should not talk at all and should not fool their visitors who pilgrimage from far-off lands, from black and white capitals. From white glass coloured capitals. From grey capitals.

ii

Nárcisz

Nárcisz's telephone call in leapmonth

The telephone is the one thing to survive it.
We can speak only briefly.
Yet from the receiver sea gulls are pouring out.
Circulating in the narrow tunnels of my ears.
And suddenly I am rolling in the salty air too.
These words are nestlings learning to fly
fluttering – some of them are bound to fall.
So let this be my contour. Washed away.
Your face is a drained watercolour.
Here it rains all the time.
I deserve it. My eyes trickle down the glass of the phone box.
I stuff the gulls, my couriers, into the phone.

Can you hear them?
Short screams. This is the message.
I would rather they shut up – slamming my hand to the receiver.
It occurs to me it is better not to hear them for you.
It is cruel I know.
I haven't got a birthday, do not call.

Nárcisz at an exhibition in Budapest

on the 50th anniversary of '56

I want to smell like them too – said Nárcisz and walked into the gallery of a hollow exhibition hall where lined up they were hanging on parallel hangers a thousand of them bleached and starched as if they were preparing for some final procession marching motionless faceless too anaemic to smile *I want to be a shirt too* – said Nárcisz in the grand chamber gesturing up at the high ceiling missing the final one pressed against the second last partially concealed for effect saturated in red paint *I want to try their beds* – said Nárcisz and jumped into the one centrally placed in the sunlit rotunda hiding under a crisp duvet patterned with photographs black and white *I want to sleep* – said Nárcisz and fell asleep on an operating table neon lit pretending to snore loudly like an aeroplane in the distant sky then to yawn inarticulately until the alarm went off *I want to be the second last instead* – said Nárcisz pressing her bleached back against the second last, her shirt concealed for effect leaving the attendant guards in the empty hall perplexed

Nárcisz's vocation in Rome

here the afternoon swifts like a moped circularly with baroque nuns babbling about *torta di mela* layer upon layer a new city a mausoleum in animation: tanned torsos panhandling on Ponte Sant' Angelo spinning in the city's rotund traffic and summer businesses on skateboards rallying their twisted bodies down looped lanes heavily gesticulating with fists maimed to captivate the visitor with cheap souvenirs; marks round the wrist and the neck

we are pushed by the spiralling crowd; en route for a three-floored abattoir, take a look at this helical world heritage, in the heat of the day Nárcisz kneels down on the elliptical floor passive violent re-enacting a fight with beasts of her hippodrome mind in the waves of a thousand thumbs down dipping her face in the sand; what are you trying to locate here? what anachronistic roars do you talk of? leave it, come on, let's go

we arrive at last to steal a glance at the face the world questions, crippled with age from the million x-rays scarred (like that beggar's at the corner look, Nárcisz, burnt in a fire!) eyes glassed-in head bowed hands frail in a marbled embrace in quiet resonances of a barrel organ sporadically floodlighting the church as tourists come and go

the assault on my back is dramatic so we both turn round Nárcisz swiftly acts wiping the gull shit off my shoulder with a fraying tissue, those sea birds come to the city early morning and cry paradoxically to the ones at the North Sea circulating above rubbish dumps, in the uproar of rotary conversations of over-crowded catacombs, while the queue is undulating slowly to the cupola of wall-papered archangels, we too decide to pursue this mosaic journey following a blindfold crowd blindfold ourselves but hush! mass is about to start; in the midst of tourists pushing and swarming a nun volunteers to conduct the humming in a Pentecostal tongue: *silence*! whispering *silenzio*, *silence s'il vous plait* and eventually *shhh*! pressing her index finger to her multilingual lips

the queue heaves on then comes to a halt underneath the ceiling another crowd frescoes a heap of open-mouthed strangers peering aloft skins inside out, pending, hooked on another sky-line; general panic, public recognition? despite the protection of muscled guard-men periodically insisting on silence and calm... Nárcisz! your time has come, your time has arrived to begin your vocation now hurry up

her vocation begins here in the flooded square in a round of applause although there are no holes in the ground to drain this enormity of rainfall so Nárcisz decides to soak outside for hours, an anorak-huddled saint musing at the colourful performance of umbrellas reflex opening and closing... lounging about from one foot to another on the red tiled roofs of a necropolis crumbling soft powder of porous tufa from under her fingernails

Nárcisz en route for memory

for my father

It seldom seeps through a thick glass. Some murky-green pond. A rough attempt. Familiar. A face water-down. It is hard to tell. The profile slurred. The truss of the bike earthed in the bottom. Could late August air melt the glass? This is January here when I pass by this pond. It is August when I stare into it. Leaning… back against the hot car. Your shirt stained with sweat. Footprints in tarmac.

(It was good to pop into the garden, you know, walking through the cathedral grounds bumping into some familiar staccato chords. Then through the gates. Louder and louder. We have made this walk before, and through the garden door across the hedges and the thorny rose bushes behind a red-bricked wall: her navy cap on. Incredible accordion on her lap. Bellows up and down.)

Sheet by sheet, we peeled the trunk of the silver birch the whole afternoon, slowly so January passed by. Numerous drafts of late summers ran down the pergamen's sun-dried skin: manuscript stretched. Scraped.

Nárcisz's breakfast letter

I will simply tell you what I can see on this table, here. No, not on that table but on the one that floats. In the window. The one that moves with the hour. Its lustrous objects, some of them latent, some obvious, layer by layer half-sheltered behind each other like a mock-up of some insipid geology, travel by the horizon. I will tell you. Although it's not easy to stop. Seeing inside. A crooked vase. Bursting flowers. They burst on the glass. I do not know what sort but not sunflowers and the vase is not blue of any kind. I could ask someone and if they did not know they could ask someone and if they did not know. Apples piled on top of each other buoyant in a bowl relatively visible: curvaceous torsos, perpendicularly squashing against one another with a negligible force unit of kilo Pascal. Though, weight nullifies for those who only watch. Did you know that despite the apparent struggle, these apples strive for equalization? They say. A kitchen knife tilted on its side. Its glossy metal edge reflects another ceiling, another sky, blurs it, blurs its white. The texture of air woven between the metal and the white escapes and floods the room. The razor's edge facing down the surface of the table reflects unknown darkness, a darkness duplicate. The intimate recollections of the two. A chunk of butter. Left outside sunbathing in the light yellow light of early afternoon melting into its own outline. Then the butter expands and steps out of itself. It becomes smeared on the glass. I read that objects have no contours, only oscillating transitions. I don't know if it is true. Perhaps the replica of it is true. An eggshell in a gaudy eggcup, its top torn off with a zigzagged motion. A mineralized minuscule skull, drained, after an elongated tribal ritual. But this time no religion, no ideology. An embroidered egg cap, a Sunday outfit. Still warm from

incubating the freshly boiled egg. If you were here you would slip into the needlework's inner textile and reel up the story of the thread stitched vice versa. If it wasn't too late. Look, these objects are travellers. Wait. Only a few more things here. A light green net bag; it is more pistachio. A fishnet fishless. Or a marionette collapsed after the hand dropped it. Yet it seems it wakes again, stretches with the stretching of the sun. It all changes by the second. Let's hurry up. It's not easy to erect a world. Outside. A jam jar with lumps of marmalade. Left open. The lid is chequered; red and white, red and white. This pattern restricted to the circle of the rim continues outside the rim too, it brims over it. Audibly. But this would be a detour and we must stay, we must stay here, with a facsimile table that'll soon depart. The table that is still here…
just…

Nárcisz's writing tablets

The red suitcase I have been travelling with for years from this island to the city, I found in a fast running stream in the wood: one of the zips has never worked but it has still been suitable for long journeys, to and fro.

After our brief hike through mountains covered with young oaks and birch trees you got worried about me catching Lyme-disease as a blood-thirsty tick attempted to tunnel its sharp jaws into my skin. You texted me to examine my entire body thoroughly in the bath. You told me you were concerned about the life of future descendants.

You repeatedly burst into inarticulate weeping at weddings, you complained. 'Well, don't fucking go to weddings then' was your friend's advice.

When I arrived home the whole country was mourning the thousand year old oak lost to the storm. At least ten people could have embraced its trunk. It was as old as the state, they said anxiously; before the election.

I wanted to flick the tiny insect off the back of my hand with my fingernail. Its hard mail with black legs flapping, the whole smart, vile, resistant. We stood at the edge of cliffs. Weightless paragliders, we soared off into the horizon. We saw the city, a stretched gigantic palm unpicking old seams of the countryside. We noticed the flesh of hills was bitten, disembowelled, geography altered. We decided to ring you about it.

The top of a traffic sign was floating on the surface of the Danube, no, not floating, sunk. Conducting massive tree trunks, roots and water corpses. The arches of the bridges filled; medieval cups turned upside down, almost spilled. Fast green currents at the gates of parliament thirsty; claiming promises.

The yellow tram gyrated like a belly dancer. Passengers at the back like waves appeared at sudden bends. They laughed and felt generous as the city musician balanced through the carriage joint that contracted, occasionally, with the greasy accordion.

Just one tea? Not two tea? asked the Dutchman at Schiphol. No, just one tea, not two, and if I may pay by pounds, please?

'Che cos'è ...?'

Nárcisz asks the question of questions

Only a river could navigate this Sunday.
One intersecting sentence in stasis.
We must go out there; walk along it holding onto
banisters that construct these late night conversations.
Is there a river in this town? Combed with bridges
arching a hiatus long-standing.

This map does not show what you want,
what side-street you arbitrarily turn into with enquiries,
incoherent. With waves hung too high. Too soft.
In a diagonal hunt for the other eavesdropping under
the architecture of the hour. Hold on. Run. It is a saying.

Nárcisz and the Magician

In and out of Guggenheim

Facing *The Poet* you laugh out loud and say 'this is what you look like' pointing at a pyramidal figure, scattered legs and arms, face sliced, unrecognisable, dissected and reconstructed human form. 'But in the end, aren't we all only lines, planes, lights and colours?' you add, hesitating at the next artwork in this geometric cavalcade: it is window-framed, hung on white wall, to and fro its edges, ferries trickle down the clear sky, a noisy market in the foreground tinted primary colours, red, yellow and patches of sea, you pull my arm to step into it, to step outside:

And we slip into a glass orb. Its transparent razors slice anyone who stares into it. It is renowned for that. A fruit tree pours out on your hair, its ruby fruits blend into your frizzy curls. Now you are dismembered too. Multiplied. Face replicated like masks that hang like autumnal leaves on every tree. On poplars and birches. None fits the expression you wear, too big, too small, too loose, only half covering what should be fully concealed, crafted from plastic or goat's skin, or simply too gluey, too untrue, too real so you latch on to the one that's safe, the one you are accustomed to instead, spit in your wine and say: it is not this place you know but the one that is yet undiscovered, the one where you have been already is the place that you could have been, where it could have happened, where it all has already happened, Campo Ruga, you sob. And we roll around again, in a centrifugal force, looking for our legs and arms, and lips and eyes drawn apart, grasping for a newer, an indisputable physique.

To watch and wait. Sitting by bridges. It may take hours, or days, sometimes months, or years, to hold the shutter. In order to catch an invisible arch becoming. The only way to do this is to wait. Until it becomes. In a whirlpool of gasoline. A bridge, complete. Until it is rolled up like a ball, a glossy ball, liquefied like the map in your hand this city reels down with meandering boats like troops of rare black swans, necks entwined, wings streamlined. You spot one. And two or three more. Sarcophagi. Sinister black coffins. You shake your head, this isn't the place that could have been. St Peter's, you whisper and you gesture at the canals that stink. 'Only if this place had not been in the way' adamant like an ocean cruiser towering over, twice the size. It chokes that tiny island, can't you see, that unknown outcrop, a comouflaged cape that quivers when it hits the side.

And we start again… on the coastline, the hide and seek, in the maze of the sea your head appears and disappears. And we dive again. The tide pulls the plane, like a submarine trip. Back home, our new home. A millennium old home. Down or up bellow sharp chains of mountains. Snowed up. Around us rain and fish. 'I always suspected him.' You sigh.

Do I remember when your squid, like an apple core got stuck in your throat? When the wine was too acidic, that it scalded your gullet, the sea too salty, you almost drowned? The city too labyrinthine and you got dizzy? Those canals on the map were not to follow, not to trust. Look, they would have never directed us to the open sea, through countless *sotoportegos*, dark *misericordia* – it isn't the place. And do I remember the baker and his cake, wrapped in the garment of the jovial local town dweller, you bet his wife and his daughter were his props, each morning, remember? The one who conjures croissants from under the glass case *like this*, in a soft white serviette, almost touching your skin, with the curved motion of the neck of the boats, the black swans, flamboyant black coffins? You never fell for his performing art, for his blue eyes that dipped into yours, when he passed it onto you, from hand to hand, and called you by your name.

The recollections of Nárcisz

Heat floods your garden; it brims over its rim
overflowing your neighbouring landscapes
dehydrating colours: an iconoclasm of summer,

a desert of your ambitions or longings. Yet you
bathe in it. You bathe and let your skin burn for
prolonged seasons until it shreds ashes and apathy.

You are cold blooded after winter. Leaning over,
face dipped in the pond you see through at last: a corrie
formed from glaciers of years' frosts, or the sky,

entrapped, iced up. You have been toiling to move on.
Chancing it with your feet, like white-washed lighthouses
near hazardous shoals, ludicrous, goose-fleshed,

you plunge. Among living things that learnt it by heart.
The distance. A short-lived echo dives after you with a
swimmer's poise and disappears as suddenly as people die.

The Shouting Girl

'to the Tihany Echo'

This may be, you wonder, this may be the place for you at last. This island is your final chance to encompass all your dislodged failures, core disorientations. This, as it seems, is another cape of the mainland, another odd dream, overlapping the one drawn on maps. You travelled far enough for this spectacle, you say, from the very West shorelines of the open sea, your firm standpoint for all discourses, lying in wait. *Pomatias elegans*: a mystery why it was so essential to visit this land, in the heart of long-forgotten Europe, to track down the traces of the old creature you only saw once for an instant, trudging in neighbouring dunes and meadows. Its yellow brown shell slender, light reddish with a colour patterned by whitish flames radially and spirally stretching upwards like Babel's dome. A tiny cone in your hand. A vital fauna element, you explain. It crawls up your palm leaving familiar pictographs of mucous on your skin. It is smart. With a door often shut to keep the world out. In.

And you pick up a goat's nail instead. Lifting it up to your ear, you listen inside its channel: you'll hear the ocean, we say. Yes, I know. There was a princess with golden-haired goats, but she was too proud and hard of heart and was punished (cursed by the king of the lake): her goats were lost in undercurrents, only their nails remained, and since then she is obliged to answer to every passers-by. Everyone remembers the Shouting Girl, the one you swear you saw. Here the landscape has changed. How could you hear her echo, the one that's long faded away? Her face eclipsed yours, you recall, with her dark red hair like this land's flora and fauna, loose and dense. A milliard years old. So we photograph your reflection in the wine cellar's moist yellow mirrors, chipped and cracked: an art nouveau city, a hazy sketch. Look: your face, flaking off too. With your fingernail you inscribe your name among other signatures in the wall of the hermits' caves, carved from porous basalt tufa: there is something that connects us, look. And connects all other places: these worlds of the catacombs, engraved in an orthodox style, are crypts of our past and future thoughts, hermits' prayer nooks, dug and hidden dialogues of overstarry nights. Their draughty tombs shelter from the heat. There once was a sea here and nothing else. Listen to the shell. Pour its contents into your ear. The umbrella you purchased locally could not wrestle with the salt and the tide. Above your head, look, in the abbey you'll find a charter you cannot read. The first record of that subterranean tongue I curse and dream in.

Only with you could I do that journey. Only with you could I go to the temple again. We have no matches, in neither of the pockets padded with sand grains and washed tissues. Come with me, you stare. Tonight, you persist, the Sun, the Earth and the Moon will stand together, synchronically. There. And we watch the darkening white of the Moon. Your head above mine in the narrow window cut in the door. Since things overlap. They eclipse. *But, look I do not believe in their tears of blood. In that golden sculpture, whose embroidered garment they change every Sunday of every week, after each miracle she performed. My eyesight has never cleared. Your hearing wore down. We can scarcely walk, we can scarcely speak. I'm sorry I am letting you down. I do not believe in magic any longer.* You are talking in the night, over it. You are talking over the dark Danube. Over the bridge arching it. In between your words tiny fireworks, suspended every ten meters in the thick black air. They are welding the bridge, pyrotechnics, reconstructing its framework, every ten meters a builder leaning over, decoding metallic hieroglyphs that flare up their face. A wild duck flies in between your last sentence and the arch. It coincides with your breath.

Yet I will go with you. I'll crawl up their serpentine paths with you. Up to the temple I will walk the walk of Kálvária. I'll come back for you next year, and we'll depart from this place, from this city. We'll depart from this bridge, where the wild duck shoots in between that oil rig and your sentence, your sentence that disappears like the cat that runs across the night of every night across an unknown town my train departs from, the two forming a V shape in the eye, passing drowsy stationmasters who guard hamlets with no name. They never gave up the task to salute. For we gain another chance to get to know the dead. An entire new life to get to know who they never were, your saints. The world, you say, has some basic shapes and forms, as we pan over the sand patterned radially and spirally by the wind and the tide. Everything else, simulation.

Yet you want to see her, you murmur. You want to simply follow her, *the woman wrapped in Sun.* It gives you strength, like the tide. Their inaudible chant. *Maria, you are beautiful indeed.* Their motionless wait for the ladder to descend again from the skies.

ACKNOWLEDGEMENTS

Special thanks to:

Denise Riley, George Szirtes
and Nathan Hamilton…

further thanks to:

my mother,
Hajnalka Lehóczky, Szabolcs Szigeti, Isabel A. Hill,
Grainne McGeough, Veronika Schandl, Anna Selby,
Janet Macpherson, Clive Sexton, Noemi Kovács, Anna Kocsis,
Marketa Mikulova, Liz Adams, Angela Pegg, Kate Kilalea,
Amaan Hyder, Tracy Angel, Hayley Buckland, Meghan Purvis,
Hayley Wilson, Jonathan Tosch, Julie Woodhead, Emil Hargittay,
Éva Szentes, Gergely Hargittay, Fiona Curran, Gabi Bazsó,
Emese Kálmán, Sarah Hesketh, Jenny Thompson, Jack Underwood,
Jennifer Oey, Jo Budd, Brian Excel, Miranda J. Lowe, Chris Hull,
Joe Kennedy, Emma Bell, Sam Riviere, Trevor Potter, Alison Mobbs,
Stephanie Leal, Annette Bowles, Ashir Abbas, David Hill, Peter Merrick,
Frances Doorman, Lynda Thompson, Melody Wright, Joel Rodker,
Alice Wright, David Crajthorne and Alexander Gordon Smith…

for their past and present assistance and for, in their various ways,
either discreetly or boisterously, believing in it.